Leeds

Leeds

Clive Hardy

Waterton Press Limited

First published in the United Kingdom in 1999 by
Frith Publishing an imprint of Waterton Press Limited.

British Library Cataloguing in Publication Data.

Clive Hardy
Leeds

ISBN 1-84125-091-0

Reproductions of all the photographs in this book are
available as framed or mounted prints. For more
information please contact The Francis Frith Collection
at the address below quoting the title of this book and
the page number and photograph number or title.

The Francis Frith Collection,
'Friths Barn', Teffont, Salisbury, Wiltshire, SP3 5QP
Tel: 01722 716376
E mail: bookprints@francisfrith.com
Web pages: www.francisfrith.com

Typeset in Bembo Semi Bold

Printed and bound in Great Britain by
WBC Limited, Bridgend, Glamorgan.

Contents

Francis Frith 1822-1898

Introduction

Francis Frith: A Victorian Pioneer

Francis Frith, the founder of the world famous photographic archive was a complex and multitudinous man. A devout Quaker and a highly successful and respected Victorian businessman he was also a flamboyant character.

By 1855 Frith had already established a wholesale grocery business in Liverpool and sold it for the astonishing sum of £200,000, equivalent of over £15,000,000 today. Now a multi-millionaire he was able to indulge in his irresistible desire to travel. As a child he had pored over books penned by early explorers, and his imagination had been stirred by family holidays to the sublime mountain regions of Wales and Scotland. "What a land of spirit-stirring and enriching scenes and places!" he had written. He was to return to these scenes of grandeur in later years to "recapture the thousands of vivid and tender memories", but with a very different purpose. Now in his thirties, and captivated by the new science of photography, Frith set out on a series of pioneering journeys to the Middle East, that occupied him from 1856 until 1860.

He took with him a specially-designed wicker carriage which acted as camera, dark-room and sleeping chamber. These far-flung journeys were full of intrigue and adventure. In his life story, written when he was sixty-three, Frith tells of being held captive by bandits, and fighting "an awful midnight battle to the very point of exhaustion and surrender with a deadly pack of hungry, wild dogs". He bargained for several weeks with a "mysterious priest" over a beautiful seven-volume illuminated Koran, which is now in the British Museum. Wearing full arab costume, Frith arrived at Akaba by camel seventy years before Lawrence of Arabia, where he encountered "desert princes and rival sheikhs, blazing with jewel-hilted swords".

During these extraordinary adventures he was assiduously exploring the desert regions of the Nile and recording the antiquities and people with his camera, Frith was the first photographer ever to travel beyond the sixth cataract. Africa, we must remember, was still the "Dark Continent", and Stanley and Livingstone's famous meeting was a decade into the future. The conditions for picture taking confound belief. He laboured for hours on end in his dark-room in the sweltering heat, while the volatile collodion chemicals fizzed dangerously in their trays. Often he was forced to work in tombs and caves where conditions were cooler.

Back in London he exhibited his photographs and was "rapturously cheered" by the Royal Society. His reputation as a photographer was made overnight. His photographs were issued in albums by James S. Virtue and William MacKenzie, and published simultaneously in London and New York. An eminent historian has likened their impact on the population of the time to that on our own generation of the first photographs taken on the surface of the moon.

Characteristically, Frith spotted the potential to create a new business as a specialist publisher of photographs. In 1860 he married Mary Ann Rosling and set out to photograph every city, town and village in Britain. For the next thirty years Frith travelled the country by train and by pony and trap, producing photographs that were keenly bought by the millions of Victorians who, because of the burgeoning rail network, were beginning to enjoy holidays and day trips to Britain's seaside resorts and beauty spots.

To meet the demand he gathered together a team of up to twelve photographers, and also published the work of independent artist-photographers of the reputation of Roger Fenton and Francis Bedford. Together with clerks and photographic printers he employed a substantial staff at his Reigate studios. To gain an understanding of the scale of Frith's business one only has to look at the catalogue issued by Frith & Co. in 1886. It runs to some 670 pages listing not only many thousands of views of the British Isles but also photographs of most major European countries, and China, Japan, the USA and Canada. By 1890 Frith had created the greatest specialist photographic publishing company in the world.

He died in 1898 at his villa in Cannes, his great project still growing. His sons, Eustace and Cyril, took over the task, and Frith & Co. continued in business for another seventy years, until by 1970 the archive contained over a third of a million pictures of 7,000 cities, towns and villages.

The photographic record he has left to us stands as a living monument to a remarkable and very special man.

Frith's dhow in Egypt *c.*1857

INTRODUCTION TO LEEDS

Leeds was the industrial powerhouse of the West Riding, and like all our great industrial cities, it grew from much humbler beginnings. When the Domesday Book was being compiled, Leeds was little more than an agricultural village huddled between the river and what is now Kirkgate. There were 35 families, a priest, a church and a mill – the latter doing well enough to be worth four shillings a year.

The village was under the lordship of Ilbert de Lacy, William the Conqueror's man in those parts, and as such appears to have escaped the wrath of the Conqueror when he laid waste to much of Yorkshire following an uprising in 1070. Around 1100 de Lacy sublet Leeds to Ralph Paganel, who was also the tenant-in-chief of Headingley and other lands throughout the county. Paganel, rich and powerful in his own right, was appointed High Sheriff of Yorkshire in 1110.

In Leeds and the surrounding villages, cloth manufacture seems to have been underway on a small scale by the twelfth century, almost certainly influenced by close proximity of the Cistercian abbey of Kirkstall. Endowed by Henry de Lacy in thanks to the Blessed Virgin, Kirkstall like the Cistercian abbeys of Fountains, Rievaulx and Jervaulx, kept huge flocks of sheep for their wool. In the twelfth century most of the wool was sold for weaving in Flanders and Northern Italy, though there was a fair amount of weaving done at both York and later Beverley, with Leeds, Wakefield, Whitby and Selby the poor relations. By the late-fourteenth century, however, times were changing. The guilds at York and Beverley were so over-regulated and over-taxed with guild levies that they were unable to rise to the challenge of cheaper textiles from the likes of Leeds, Halifax and Wakefield, where production costs were lower. Even so, as late as 1470 Leeds was still being described as "near Rothwell". Yet within the next 50 years the town would emerge as the leading centre in Yorkshire for the trade in woollen cloths, and by 1560 was probably similar in size to Bradford. There were houses on both sides of Briggate as far as the Headrow, and others beyond Timble Bridge over Sheepscar Beck. The population at this time would have been around 3,000 if the outlying hamlets of Woodhouse, Buslingthorpe, Potternewton and Knowsthorpe are taken into consideration.

By 1612 the population had probably doubled, due in part to people coming to the town in search of work. Building development now extended along Kirkgate, Boar Lane, Vicar Lane and Swinegate: an ever-growing mixture of housing and workshops as Leeds' position within the textile industry continued to strengthen. The town was no longer simply engaged in manufacturing: it had become the leading finishing centre in the West Riding for cropping, dyeing and dressing. Leeds merchants traded aggressively both at home and abroad, securing markets previously dominated by the merchants of York, Beverley and Hull.

In January 1643, Sir William Savile entered Leeds at the head of a Royalist force of 500 horsemen and 1,500 foot soldiers. Savile then set about fortifying the town: artillery was sited to cover Briggate, earthworks were thrown up at the north end of Leeds Bridge and a trench was dug around the town perimeter to the banks of the Aire. On 23rd January, Sir Thomas Fairfax at the head of a Parliamentarian force of 3,000 men, crossed the Aire at Apperley Bridge and halted on Woodhouse Moor. Sir Thomas followed the rules of engagement of the day by offering Sir William terms. Sir William declined and the assault began at around 2pm. Within two hours the Parliamentarians had broken through the defences and the battle was soon over. Though Sir William escaped, 500 of his men were taken prisoner but as was the custom, they were allowed to go free after promising to take no further part in the war.

In 1646 Charles I was held prisoner for one night at the Red Hall in Upper Head Row. One of the stories surrounding the king's short stay in Leeds concerns John Harrison, a wealthy landowner. On hearing that the king was being held in Leeds, Harrison asked permission to meet with him and present him with a tankard of ale. The king accepted Harrison's offer and on opening the lid of the tankard found it full of golden guineas which "his Majesty did, with much celerity, hasten to secrete about his royal person".

∽ Powerhouse of West Riding ∽

By 1600 Leeds had established itself as the most important of all the cloth fairs in the county. Every Tuesday and Saturday tables were set up on the bridge over the Aire at the bottom of Briggate. When the market bell tolled the sellers would move to the tables, which they had to share, and stand in line behind their pieces. The traders entered when the bell stopped tolling. Business was done in a whisper so that other buyers and sellers could not overhear the price agreed. After a couple of hours the bell tolled to signal the end of the market and everything was cleared away. Daniel Defoe reckoned that in a morning somewhere between £10,000-£20,000 worth of cloth was traded.

By 1710 these open-air markets were being challenged by Cloth Halls, where business could be done whatever the weather outside. Leeds answered the challenge in 1711 with the opening of a hall for White Cloths. In 1755 a new and much larger purpose-built White Cloth Hall was opened, followed a few months later by a Mixed Cloth Hall.

By 1775 the population of Leeds is thought to have been about 17,000 and by the time of the first census of 1801 it had rocketed to 53,000. The coming of the factory system led to thousands leaving the countryside in search of work. The work they found was alien to them: strict discipline, regular attendance, long hours and unsafe working practices. Yorkshire mill owners were at the forefront when it came to employing child labour in almost slave-like conditions. Many of these children were sent north from London workhouses. Those who ended up in the mills around Leeds were luckier than the children sent to Bradford. In Leeds they worked a 12-hour day; in Bradford, 13. In both places children were beaten to keep them awake.

With the factory system came machinery. As with every subsequent generation, the factory workers of the early-nineteenth century equated mechanisation with the threat to jobs. In the 1800s reaction to the threat manifested itself in the movement that came to be known as Luddism. The earliest cases in Yorkshire date from 1811 to 1812 when croppers rebelled against the introduction of shearing frames.

West Yorkshire's most famous Luddite was George Mellor. On 6th January 1813, George Mellor, William Thorpe and Thomas Smith were indicted before the grand jury at York Castle with the wilful murder of William Horsfall, merchant and manufacturer. With a former accomplice Benjamin Walker turning king's evidence, they had little chance and were executed at York. A few days later seven men went on trial charged with attacking William Cartwright's mill. Cartwright had already taken the precaution of arranging for troops to help guard his mill. When the Luddites attacked the troops opened fire. In an attack lasting about 20 minutes, both sides exchanged fire and several men died of their wounds. Found guilty, the Luddites were sentenced to death and executed at York.

It was the combination of the factory system and the application of steam power that led to the concentration of textile production in a handful of towns, including Bradford, Huddersfield, Dewsbury, Batley, Bingley and Leeds. By the mid-nineteenth century there was an enormous diversity in the manufacturing base of the town. Though woollens still dominated the scene, the flax industry employed over 9,000 workers and other industries included rope, glass, earthenware and paper manufacturing.

Coalmining was a major industry in the area. At its height there were 102 collieries employing 5,000 miners and with an annual total output of 2.5 million tons. Engineering also played an important part in the development of Leeds. Fairbairn & Lawson manufactured flax and tow machinery, much of which went for export.

The area also became a centre for the manufacture of railway locomotives, with such firms as Todd, Kitson & Laird, Fenton, Murray & Jackson, and EB Wilson & Co. When EB Wilson & Co closed in the 1850s much of the equipment and patterns were purchased by Manning, Wardle & Co, with the result that Manning's early locomotives looked like EB Wilson products.

In 1860 yet another locomotive manufacturer appeared on the scene with the opening of Hudswell, Clarke & Co, followed in 1864 by the Hunslet Engine Co. The latter would be the last of the Leeds locomotive builders to remain in business, surviving into the 1990s.

By the 1850s, Kitson's Airedale foundry was turning out traction, stationary and ploughing engines for John Fowler, though Fowler eventually opened his own works.

Later still, Samuel Fox developed pressed-steel railway bogies and wagon underframes. Though Leeds had become a major engineering centre, iron-making was always on a small scale and even in 1871 there were only two blast furnaces in the borough. There were, however, a large number of foundries, such as the Leeds Forge Co and Kirkstall Forge Co, producing all manner of castings. Towards the end of the nineteenth century the production of wrought iron declined as steel gained in popularity. Most firms switched to using steel imported from Middlesborough, Sheffield and Rotherham.

In the 1870s, Leeds was a smoke-covered, overcrowded dump. Three-quarters of the population was crammed into one-eighth of the area of the borough, in some of the most appalling housing in existence. As more and more people had flocked to Leeds in search of work, cheap housing had been thrown up to accommodate them, often without any thought being given to sewage disposal or water supply. The result was that infectious diseases were often rife in working-class areas: cholera epidemics killed 700 in 1832 and over 2,000 in 1848-49. The tourist attraction in Wellington Yard in 1872 was a midden 6 ft deep, 6 ft wide and 21 ft long, and God help anyone who fell in it.

There had been little or no regulation regarding the building of workers' housing. For example, Johnson's Square was 15 single-room houses situated below the level of Charles Street; Camp Field off Water Lane comprised 92 back-to-back houses built in an area of just 70yds by 125yds. Another feature of local housing was the blind-backs, which had no rear windows or doors. From the end elevation they looked like a house that had been cut in half and one half pulled down. Some blind-backs were built up against factory walls, others were built so that they looked like ordinary houses from the outside with a central porch. In fact, these were two blind-backs, each consisting of four single-room houses, probably accommodating 30 or more people.

It has been estimated that by 1881 around 80 per cent of England's population was now living in towns, compared with only 25 per cent in 1800. Though Leeds continued to play a major role in the woollen industry, competition was increasing and several large mills diversified into dyeing and finishing. By the 1891 census the textile industry was employing 22,313 workers, a slight reduction over 1881, but clothing manufacturing had nearly doubled to 30,172 employees. Over the period 1881-1891, an additional 23,000 manufacturing and 32,000 transport, professional and service-sector jobs had been created in Leeds, and the total population had risen from 309,835 to 366,129. Still Leeds continued to grow. By 1901 the population stood at 428,744 and by 1911 it was 445,791. It was all far removed from the tiny hamlet of 1085.

∽ By Road ∞

Leeds rise to one of the leading industrial centres in the country was also due in part to the development of transport and communication links not only throughout West Yorkshire but with Lancashire, the Midlands, the north-east and London. By the mid-eighteenth century what passed for the existing road network was under severe strain, unable to cope with increasing and often heavy freight traffic generated by the expanding woollen industry, collieries and agriculture. The two principal turnpikes in the area were the Leeds to Ripon via Harrogate, and the Leeds to Skipton. Turnpikes offered a system of reasonably well-maintained roads for the first time since the Roman occupation. In the 1750s the journey from Leeds to London took at least four days. By the end of the eighteenth century, thanks to turnpikes, it took just over one day. Turnpikes enabled scheduled daily stagecoach services to operate, strengthening the town's links with York, Hull, Sheffield, Manchester, Birmingham, Carlisle and London. The Leeds-to-Bradford turnpike was one of the busiest, carrying large quantities of freight as well as passenger traffic. In 1778 tolls on this road amounted to £852; by 1798 the sum was £2,843 and in 1810 it had risen to £4,445.

By 1830 Leeds was one of the busiest coaching interchanges in the provinces, with well over 100 daily scheduled services leaving the coaching inns in Briggate. Both long-distance and short-haul freight services were operated to and from Leeds, the town having no less than 180 haulage businesses, many of which had their offices in local inns, where business could be done over a bottle of brandy or a few jugs of ale.

In 1835 coaching was at its peak with around 3,300 stagecoaches and over 700 mail coaches operating daily scheduled services. However the writing was already on the wall. As early as 1830 the Post Office had contracted the Liverpool & Manchester Railway to carry mail.

∽ By Water ∞

In November 1700, the Aire and Calder was open for navigation as far as Leeds Bridge, where a wharf and a warehouse had been built on the north bank. Cloth could now be loaded for Hull, London, the Baltic and the Low Countries. The obvious advantage that water transport had over the roads was that of cost. It was far cheaper to send 20 tons of coal to Hull by way of the Aire and Calder than it was to hire sufficient wagons to do the same job.

By 1760 river navigation was possible to Elland and Halifax, but the real prize would be the linking of the Humber with the Mersey. In 1770 the Leeds & Liverpool Canal was sanctioned. At 127 miles in length excluding branches, the canal was the longest in Britain. The first section, Bingley to Skipton, was opened by 1773 and in 1777 the sections from Aire and Calder at Leeds to Gargrave, and from Wigan to Liverpool were open for traffic. Then the money ran out. In 1790 a new Act allowed funds to be raised for construction of the middle section, but following the outbreak of war with France the funding slowed down and it was not until 1816 that the canal was open throughout.

One of the problems suffered by the Leeds & Liverpool was lack of adequate water supplies. In long dry summers some sections had to be closed for weeks at a time and despite the heavy payloads capable of being carried, carriers were forced to seek a reliable alternative.

∽ By Rail ∾

In June 1758 the Middleton Railway became the first in Britain to be sanctioned under an Act of Parliament. Built to a gauge of 4 ft 1 in, the Middleton ran to a coal staith south of Leeds Bridge. The staith was built to supply the town at a guaranteed price of just over 10s a ton. Other collieries in the area were unable to compete and as a result Middleton had a virtual monopoly on the coal sold in Leeds.

The Middleton was worked by horses until 1812 when steam locomotives made an appearance. Steam traction continued until 1835 when horses once again took over. Steam locomotives were reintroduced in 1866 and the line converted to standard gauge in 1881.

Main-line railways came to the Leeds area in 1834 with the opening of the Leeds & Selby line. The effect upon the Aire and Calder Navigation was almost immediate and the company had little alternative but to slash its freight charges in an attempt to remain competitive. By 1840 the Leeds & Selby line had been extended to Hull and a direct rail link with the Midlands had been opened, thanks to the North Midland Railway line to Derby, where there was an end-on connection with the Derby & Birmingham. At this time, the Leeds & Manchester Railway did not run directly into town but connected with the North Midland at Normanton.

In 1846 the Leeds & Bradford line opened, followed in 1848 by the London & North Western line. In 1849 Headingley and Horsforth were linked by rail to Leeds with the opening of the Leeds Northern to Harrogate. On the eve of the railway amalgamations of 1st January 1923, Leeds was at the centre of a comprehensive railway network and served by five railway companies: the London & North Western, the Midland, the North Eastern, the Lancashire & Yorkshire, and the Great Northern. There were passenger stations at Wellington Street, Leeds Central and Leeds New. Goods facilities were at Wellington Street, Cardigan Road, Hunslet Lane and Central.

CHAPTER 1

∽ LEEDS ∾

Many of the pictures in this collection date from around 1900 when Leeds was not only a great engineering centre, but the very hub of the cloth industry. In 1901 the population stood at 428,953 making Leeds the first city in Yorkshire and the fifth in England.

TOWN HALL, *c.*1965.

L28066

When this picture was taken, the town hall was in desperate need of a good clean to rid it of decades worth of soot, grime and bird muck. In 1972 it was at last listed to be cleaned but this was the only item, other than the sale of council houses, to which the Labour group on the council objected.

VICTORIA HALL, 1888. 20984

The town hall not only housed the council: there were law courts, facilities for lectures, holding public meetings and for music festivals. This is the Victoria Hall, the stage area dominated by the organ.

TOWN HALL AND THE HEADROW, c.1955. L28004

In 1950 the wool industry was still important to Yorkshire, where 1,123 woollen and worsted mills employed around 150,000. By 1967 there were 825 mills in operation, but by 1986 the figure had dropped to 172.

TOWN HALL, 1894.
When Leeds town hall was opened by Queen Victoria, the streets were lined with palm trees and triumphal arches. Designed by Cuthbert Broderick the building with its classical lines symbolised Leeds position as the leading city of West Riding.

WAR MEMORIAL AND THE HEADROW, *c.*1955. L28005

During the First World War, Leeds contributed over 90,000 men to the forces, of whom 9,640 were killed in action. The greatest single loss on one day occurred on 1st July 1916 during the Somme offensive when the Leeds Pals suffered horrendous casualties and were all but wiped out.

THE HEADROW, *c.*1965. L28137

This thoroughfare is a continuation of Westgate and Park Lane, and at 80 ft wide is 10 ft wider than Union Street, Aberdeen.

THE HEADROW, *c*.1965.   L28093

There was consternation for the owners of fast cars at the end of 1965 when the government introduced the 70mph speed limit. It was supposed to be for an experimental period only but has never been lifted.

CITY CENTRE, *c*.1965.   L28135

The Post Office was built on the site of the old Mixed Cloth Hall, which was opened in 1756. By the early eighteenth century, enclosed Cloth Halls in other parts of the county were taking away business from Leeds. A hall for white cloths was opened in Kirkgate in 1711, but was replaced by a larger one in 1755.

POST OFFICE AND REVENUE OFFICE, 1897.
The postal service in Victorian times was considered vital to the public good, and offices in major cities had long opening hours.

39088

20

CITY SQUARE, *c.*1965. L28085

At the beginning of the twentieth century a room at the Queen's Hotel cost 4*s* a night, breakfast 3*s* and dinner 5*s*. The Great Northern and the Metropole hotels were similarly priced, but the Grand Central in Briggate offered rooms from 4*s* 6*d* and dinner at 3s 6*d*.

CITY SQUARE, *c.*1965. L28130

On the right is the entrance to Leeds City station. At one time there were three railway stations in the city centre: Central, Wellington and New. In the late 1930s Wellington and New stations were combined and eventually rebuilt as Leeds City, while Central closed in 1967.

BLACK PRINCE STATUE, *c.*1955.   L28015

This statue is of Edward of Woodstock, better known as the Black Prince on account of his black armour. The son of Edward III, he was already a seasoned warrior at the age of 16. He made his name at Crecy in 1346 and commanded Edward's forces at Poitiers in 1356, a battle in which the French king was captured.

BOAR LANE, *c.*1965.   L28148

A Morris Minor heads along Boar Lane towards the City Square. Introduced in 1948 the Minor has since become a classic car enjoying a cult following. The Marina, introduced in 1971, was the British Leyland replacement for the Minor and the Morris Oxford.

BOAR LANE, *c.*1965.   L28146

Just a few minutes walk from here, the Leeds & Liverpool Canal links up with the River Aire and the Aire & Calder Navigation, providing Leeds with an inland waterway from the Mersey to the Humber.

DUNCAN STREET, *c*.1955.   L28011

The junction of Boar Lane and Briggate, looking towards the Corn Exchange. In the seventeenth century Leeds held its cloth fairs at the bottom end of Briggate every Tuesday and Saturday. This was the most important fair in the whole of Yorkshire, attracting traders and customers from miles away. The stalls were set up on the old bridge that spanned the Aire.

BOAR LANE, *c*.1965.   L28147

Partially hidden behind C&A is the Georgian edifice of Holy Trinity church, completed in 1727.

BRIGGATE, *c.*1965.   L28142

One of the highlights of shopping along Briggate was the glass-roofed arcades, such as the Queen's and the County.

NEW BRIGGATE, *c.*1955.   L28001

At the beginning of the twentieth century Leeds had four theatres, including The Grand, which is featured on the right-hand side of the picture. The others were The Royal in Land's Lane, The Queen's in Meadow Road and the Empire Palace in Briggate.

BRIGGATE, *c.*1955.   L28010

Trams rattle along Briggate in this picture. Leeds was one of the pioneers of segregated tracks, keeping trams and other vehicles apart. The routes to Roundhay, Belle Isle, Middleton, Temple Newsom and Lawnswood were mainly segregated systems and as such were extremely efficient.

BRIGGATE, *c.*1965.   L28089

Still the principle street for shopping, retail outlets included Henry's, Fosters, Paige & Co, and Boots. Also along here were Willerbys and GM Brown's, formerly Lawrence's International Furnishers.

BRIGGATE, c.1955.
On the left is Leeds' oldest shop, which dates from 1613 and is receiving a facelift. Further along the street on the right stands the Empire Theatre.

CIVIC HALL, *c.*1965.
The civic hall was designed by E Vincent Harris and opened with much ceremony in 1933, with temporary stands being erected for spectators. Behind and to the left are some of the buildings of the Central Colleges.

L28065

29

PARISH CHURCH, 1891.

28281

There are no medieval churches in Leeds. The church of St John the Evangelist was consecrate in 1634 and retains its oaken interior and a great screen considered to be one of the finest of its type in England. St Peter's in Kirkgate was noted for its fifteenth-century brasses, whilst eighteenth-century Holy Trinity in Boar Lane had perhaps the most attractive-looking spire in the area.

ST JOHN'S CHURCH, 1897.

39094

The seventeenth-century box pews were irreparably damaged in the "restoration" of the 1860s, when they were cut down. On the left is the two-deck pulpit and tester.

GRAMMAR SCHOOL, 1888.   20993

The earliest mention for the provision of education in Leeds dates from 1552 when William Sheafield, chantry priest of St Catherine, left property to support the upkeep of a schoolmaster. This was the beginnings of Leeds Grammar School.

COOKRIDGE STREET, c.1955.
A view of Leeds Mechanics' Institute. In June 1840 Thomas Cook arranged a members' excursion to York by way of the Leeds & Selby and the York & North Midland Railways. The trip was priced at half the normal fare and included tea at York. There were 570 passengers on what is thought to be the earliest-known excursion offered at an all-in rate.

L28008

YORKSHIRE COLLEGE, 1894. 34767

This was part of the Victoria University, which was constituted in 1880, the other colleges being at Manchester and Liverpool. The colleges went their separate ways in 1904, each becoming an independent university.

YORKSHIRE COLLEGE, 1894. 34768

One of the college's more interesting pupils was Joseph Wright who had begun working at Salt's Mill, Saltaire when he was just seven years old. Joseph studied at Yorkshire College and gained entrance to Heidleburg University. He eventually became Professor of Contemporary Philology at Oxford.

New Medical Hall, 1894. 34770

In 1652 Parliament was petitioned without success for the building of a university at York. The earliest part of Leeds University may be said to date from 1831 with the opening of the Leeds Medical School. In 1884 it was amalgamated with the Yorkshire College of Science and became part of Victoria University.

CLOTH WORKERS COURT, LEEDS UNIVERSITY, *c*.1960.   L28112
The university launched an appeal in 1925 for £500,000 to build a new medical school, departmental buildings, library and student union. Lord Brotherton donated his collection of rare books and gave £100,000 in cash. Some of the buildings were finished before the start of the Second World War, but the new central block was not completed until 1951.

UNION, REFECTORY AND TEXTILE BUILDINGS, LEEDS UNIVERSITY, *c*.1960.   L28122
When Victoria University broke up in 1904, Leeds was by far the poor relation, unable to match the financial input enjoyed by Manchester and Liverpool. In the words of Edward Baines Leeds was "a quieter, slower town and our neighbourhood is quieter".

THE BAR, UNION BUILDINGS, *c*.1965.   L28129

This photo was taken in the days of Watney's draught red barrel and "a Double Diamond Works Wonders" advertising. The only lager on sale was bottled, usually Lowenbrau.

THE ENGINEERING BUILDING, *c*.1960.   L28121

One of the university's architecturally more interesting buildings is the Brotherton Library, paid for by Lord Brotherton and containing over 500,000 volumes, including its benefactor's private collection of rare books.

LEEDS INFIRMARY, 1894.　34769

In March 1809 Mary Bateman, a resident of Leeds, was executed at York. Her body was then taken to the General Infirmary at Leeds where it was exhibited at a charge of 3d a head. Over 2,500 people paid to see her body. Later it was dissected and, following a Yorkshire custom, her skin was tanned and distributed in small pieces to those who applied.

THE PARKINSON BUILDING, *c.*1960.
This building, which was part of Leeds University, was designed by TA Lodge and opened in 1951.

L28099

ROUNDHAY PARK LAKE, 1897.
Along with Woodhouse Moor to the north, the park was considered the chief lungs of the city, where for a few hours at the weekend factory workers had an opportunity to get away from the dust, grime, noise and smell of the workplace.

39092

ROUNDHAY PARK, 1897.

In 1891 the first experiments in England using overhead wiring for electric trams, took place on the Roundhay Park route. There were problems caused by the tramway using an earth return for the traction current, so the line opened using steam tram engines. The electrified route between Kirkstall and Roundhay opened in August 1897.

ROUNDHAY PARK, 1897.

Roundhay Park was purchased by the council in 1872. It comprised 775 acres, including woodlands, lakes and a manor house, part of which was turned into refreshment rooms.

THE DRINKING FOUNTAIN, ROUNDHAY PARK, c.1960.
The council paid £139,000 for the park in 1872, it being one of a number of acquisitions by the authority over the previous 20 years. In 1852 following an outbreak of cholera, the council bought out the private water suppliers for £250,000 and embarked on schemes totalling £4 million, so that by 1918 the city was being supplied with 16 million gallons of fresh water a day. In 1870 the council also acquired control of the Gas Company for £750,000.

42

WOODHOUSE MOOR, 1897.   39096

When given the chance, people escaped from Leeds to foreign parts. In 1841 Thomas Cook organised the earliest-known Sunday excursion with a trip from Leeds to Hull. The train comprised 40 carriages and carried 1,250 passengers.

WOODHOUSE MOOR, 1897.   39095

In 1893 a study by a German sociologist found that six out of every seven working-class families in the mill towns of Lancashire and Yorkshire managed to save enough money to spend on a holiday. The money included wages earned by children.

TEMPLE NEWSAM GARDENS, c.1960.

Temple Newsam was bought by Leeds Corporation in 1922 from Edward Wood, the future Lord Halifax. The first house known to have been built here belonged to Thomas, Lord Darcy, who was executed for his involvement in the Yorkshire uprising against the Dissolution. His estate was confiscated by the Crown and later given to Margaret Tudor and her husband the Earl of Lennox. Their son married Mary, Queen of Scots.

L28050F

CHAPTER 2

∽ HEADINGLEY ∽

Headingley was once a small village to the north of Leeds and its population in 1775 was estimated at 667 people. However, like Leeds the population had doubled by 1801 and continued to rise dramatically over the coming decades.

More than half of Headingley was at one time owned by the Earl of Cardigan and it was the enclosure of the moor at Far Headingley that had led to its development. After 1821 the village expanded due to the opening of several textile factories nearby and for people working at Kirkstall. But Headingley was an attractive proposition for a growing middle class able to escape the appalling conditions in Leeds. Those who could afford to get out of Leeds were moving to the leafy northern suburbs. Linked to Leeds by rail, horse-drawn omnibus and tram, Headingley's appeal to the middle classes went into decline after the 1890s, when workers houses were built there. However, by 1901 the population stood at 41,561.

OTLEY ROAD, c.1960.

L28026

No town centre worth its salt was complete without a Co-op store. One of the great occasions in the Co-op year was going to collect the family dividend, or divi. Every family had a membership number against which all transactions were logged. The divi was the membership share of what would have been a retailer's profit after all expenses. The divi varied from one society to another and could be anything from 1s 6d to 3s in the pound.

HEADINGLEY, 1894.

34773

It would be a few years before electric street-trams would link Headingley with Leeds city centre. However, in this year Leeds corporation took advantage of the Tramways Act of 1870 and bought out the private tramway operators for over £100,000. Horse-drawn trams were replaced on some routes by steam power and electric cars were introduced from 1897.

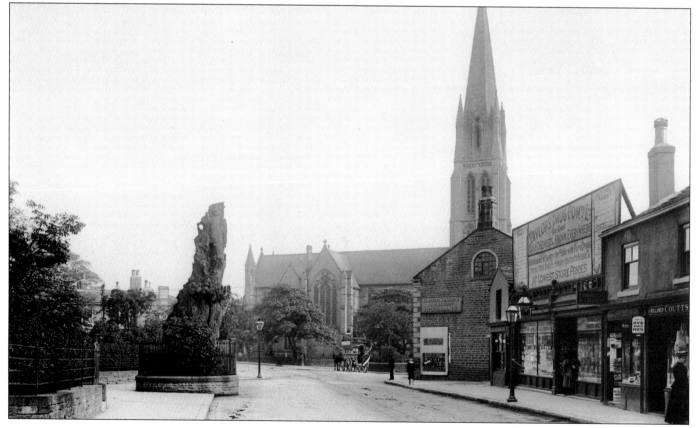

PARISH CHURCH AND OLD OAK, 1897.

39097

A view of Headingley parish church with the remains of the famous Shire Oak, which has a girth of 29 ft.

PARISH CHURCH, NAVE EAST, 1891.   28263
There were several modern churches considered to be "of a good style and would be notable in any surroundings".
The others were the Roman Catholic cathedral, St Martin's Potternewton, St John's Holbeck and Hook Memorial
Church.

HEADINGLEY COLLEGE, 1894. 34772

In the latter part of the nineteenth century, several colleges run by various religious denominations opened around Leeds. The Leeds Clergy school and the Roman Catholic Seminary were both opened in 1876. The Roman Catholic College dates from 1909, whilst the Wesleyan College at Headingley predates them all, being opened in 1868.

ST CHAD'S CHURCH, FAR HEADINGLEY, c.1960. L28033

Chad was a Northumbrian monk appointed bishop of Ite Mercians in 669. He built his cathedral at Lichfield where he died of plague in 672. Chad converted two sons of King Wulfhere of Mercia to Christianity. Wulfhere put both sons to death.

PARISH CHURCH, LADY CHAPEL, 1891.   28264

The chapel was dedicated to the Virgin Mary. In the Lady Chapel of St Edward's at Clifford, there is a statue of the Virgin sculptured by H Hoffman. Hoffman was a Jew who converted to the Catholic faith when carving the image in his studio in Rome.

CRICKET GROUND PAVILION, 1897.
Originally a part of the Cardigan Fields estate, Headingley was put on the market in 1888 and purchased by the Yorkshire County Cricket Club.

CHAPTER 3

∞ HORSFORTH ∞

This town remained independent until the local government reorganisation of 1974. Along with Pudsey, Yeadon, Aireborough, Otley, Harewood, Bardsey, Linton, Wetherby, Boston Spa, Aberford, Garforth, Ledsham, Rothwell and Morley, it became a part of the City of Leeds Metropolitan District. Even before 1974 other areas, such as Roundhay in 1912, Middleton in 1919, Adel in 1925 and Temple Newsam in 1927, had been incorporated into ever-expanding Leeds.

TOWN STREET, *c.*1960.

Throughout the 1950s and 60s the standard of living continued to rise. People could afford washing machines, fridges, televisions and cars. Annual car sales rocketed from 135,000 in 1950 to 820,000 in 1960.

THE GREEN, c.1965.
Horse power of a different kind waits outside the Black Bull, their drivers however still enjoy a refreshing pint or two of Tetley's fine ales.

Town Street, 1901.

Here we see that the horses have their nosebags on and there are no prizes for guessing where their drivers are.

47133

SHOPPING IN TOWN STREET, *c*.1965

H118094

This was the period when few supermarkets existed and those that did were built in town centres, as most people relied on public transport.

NEW ROAD SIDE, *c*.1960.

H118049

Cinema in 1960 was still a popular form of entertainment, though television and the opportunities opened up by private car ownership were both beginning to make inroads. By the late-1960s many cinemas had been converted to bingo halls (the technology was not yet available for effective multi-screen cinema complexes).

TOWN STREET, c.1965.

Even in the 1990s there are plenty of people around who can remember their Co-op numbers and going to collect their divis. You could even earn divi from your dead relatives, providing you used the Co-op funeral service, which included a ham tea send-off.

MECHANICS' INSTITUTE, 1901.
Such institutions had spread rapidly during the nineteenth century and provided workers with an opportunity to undertake education courses backed up with examinations.

47134

RING ROAD ROUNDABOUT, *c.*1960.   H118026
In 1934 Leeds City council embarked on a programme to clear 30,000 slums. Delayed by the outbreak of the Second World War, the programme continued in the 1940s and included plans to build 53,000 new homes. However, building always lagged behind demand.

SPRINGFIELD HOSPITAL, 1901.   47149
Within the Leeds township, hospital provision was pretty dire with Leeds Infirmary handling the bulk of care until the building of St James's Hospital in 1874. In the 1890s isolation hospitals were opened at Seacroft and Killingbeck.

47144

WOODSIDE CHURCH, 1901.
Among the more colourful sects to establish themselves in Leeds were the Swedenborgians and the Inghamites. The Swedenborgians arrived in 1816 but struggled to survive and were without a minister for nigh on 50 years. The Inghamites, once a force to be reckoned with in the Leeds area, declined throughout the 1870s and 80s, and finally disbanded in the 1890s.

WOODSIDE WESLEYAN CHAPEL, 1901.   47145

Between 1840 and 1885 only one new Wesleyan chapel was opened in Leeds: at Roscoe Place in 1861. Wesleyan membership declined within Leeds during the 1840s and 50s but seems to have held up in the surrounding townships, such as Horsforth. New missions to these places led to a spate of chapel building in the late-nineteenth century.

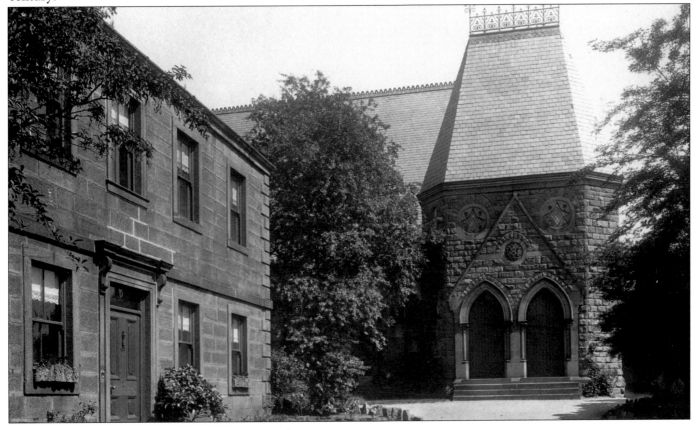

WESLEYAN CHAPEL, 1901.   47138

The Wesleyans were the first to open a college in the Leeds area: at Headingly in 1868. In 1816 they had opened the first night school, which consisted of four Sunday-school classrooms where young men aged 15 and over could attend and learn to read and write. Secular education for most children in the Leeds area was carried out by local Sunday schools until the Education Act of 1870.

NEWLAY WOOD, 1901. 47147

Within the Leeds city boundary most of the open areas between the townships gradually disappeared under an urban sprawl of industrial and housing development. Horsforth survived as an independent borough until 1974, when it was swallowed up in the City of Leeds Metropolitan District.

HORSFORTH HALL, 1901.   47139

Domestic staff in such places often worked six and a half days a week, and even on their half day off they were expected to be in by 9pm. On Sundays attendance at church was obligatory, even if you were on your half-day off.

HALL PARK, 1901.   47140

A typical complement of indoor staff would include a butler, housekeeper, governess, footman, parlourmaid, several housemaids, cook, kitchen and scullery maids. Outdoor staff would include a head gardener and any number of under gardeners and labourers.

47137

RAWDON CHURCH, 1901.

The oldest surviving churches date from Saxon times. St John, Kirk Hammerton is complete, though now forms the south aisle of a late–Victorian church. All Saints at Ledsham is also Saxon but with a number of fifteenth–century adornments.

Chapter 4

∽ Kirkstall Abbey ∽

Henry de Lacy, Lord of Pontefract, was seriously ill and was expected to die. If he survived Henry promised to build a monastery in honour of the Blessed Virgin. Well, he did survive and he kept his promise. Henry gave the abbot of Fountains Abbey land to build on at Barnoldswick. The abbot for the new Cistercian House came from Skelldale, near Ripon, but the new site did not work out and Abbot Alexander decided that he and his brethren should move somewhere else. The site they chose was Kirkstall.

Kirkstall like other Cistercian Houses grew rich on wool and the abbey is thought to have been awarded the charter to hold Wibsey Fair, one of the oldest in England. In order to finance their ever-grander building projects, the Cistercians were quite willing to sell wool for several years ahead by means of advanced contracts. Sometimes building costs and income did not balance. In 1275 Fountains Abbey had to be bailed out of its financial difficulties by the Jews of York. The abbey was in the red to the tune of £6,000, a phenomenal amount of money in those days.

VIEW OF THE ABBEY FROM THE WEIR, 1891.   28284

After the Dissolution the abbey was left a ruin and many of its stones were eventually carted off and used to widen the old Leeds Bridge. Even so the chapter house, cloisters and abbot's lodging are still impressive.

KIRKSTALL ABBEY, 1891.
The abbey played a part in the industrial development of Leeds, for it was here that iron forging first began in the district. The abbey was founded in 1152 as a daughter house of Fountains Abbey. Building work was completed by 1175 and iron forging began in 1200.

THE NAVE, c.1955.
Both Henry de Lacy and his son Robert were buried at Kirkstall.

K40003F

WESTERN FACADE, 1861.

Kirkstall grew rich on sheep and wool. In 1292 the quality of Kirkstall-raised wool was such that the abbey was able to sell its output for the next 10 years by means of a forward contract. Advance payments on these contracts enabled the monasteries to carry out their grand building schemes.

KIRKSTALL ABBEY, 1891.   28289

Cleanliness in the twelfth and thirteenth centuries was certainly not next to Godliness. The Cistercians, like the Knights Templar, were not noted for their standards of personal hygiene and rarely washed. At Kirkstall the monks had the benefit of piped water so that they might wet, rather than wash their hands before entering the refectory. There was also a bath, but its use was probably limited. The Catholic Church considered bathing in public to be sinful, though taking the waters at holy wells to relieve aches and pains was acceptable. This was because the Church controlled most of the holy wells and took a cut of the revenues.

70

KIRKSTALL CHURCH, 1894.

Three miles north-east of Kirkstall is Adel, the location of St John Baptist, the most complete Norman church in Yorkshire. Inside is a superb Norman chancel arch of three orders, of which the capitals depicting the baptism of Christ and the crucifixion were carved in situ.

34775

CHAPTER 5

∞ WETHERBY ∞

On the extreme north-eastern edge of the City of Leeds Metropolitan District, Wetherby was once an important stop-over and relay station for stagecoaches travelling the Great North Road. With the coming of the railways, long-distance stagecoach travel quickly became a thing of the past. Wetherby went into decline, relying on tourist traffic instead of scheduled coaches.

HIGH STREET, 1909. 61730
The Angel Hotel was one of three hotels that catered for motorists, the others being the George and Dragon, and the Brunswick.

NORTH STREET, 1909.

Ward & Sons was established in 1868 and had probably been smiths and/or farriers until deciding to concentrate on repairing vehicles and selling bicycles. As can be seen from the picture, it was also the local agent for the AA. Further down the street Continental Motors is the local agent for Michelin.

MARKET PLACE, 1909.
At the turn of the century Wetherby was described in some tourist guides as "a town of no interest". In 1920 all the influential Dunlop Guide had to say about the place was that it had "pleasant walks by the river".

61729

CHAPTER 6

∽ BOSTON SPA & YORKSHIRE WOOLLEN DISTRICT ∽

In 1744 a man named John Shires discovered a saline spring and given the eighteenth century fashion for taking the waters, Boston Spa was born. If Boston ever had its moment of glory it was brief enough for hardly anyone to notice. Boston, like numerous other minor Yorkshire spas, could not hope to compete with the likes of Harrogate and Scarborough, and lacked the social life that went on at Ilkley and Malton.

The Yorkshire Woollen District included within its boundaries Wakefield, Osset, Castleford, Normanton, Pontefract, Dewsbury, Batley, Birstall, Heckmondwicke and Morley. Though the woollen industry dominated the area, there was also a substantial coalmining presence, especially around the towns of Castleford and Pontefract. There were other industries too, including chemicals, engineering and glassmaking.

The geography of the district, which at its greatest dimensions is approximately 22 miles wide by nine or ten miles deep, differs between east and west. The western area is noted for its deep valleys along which the mill towns were established. The eastern area is much flatter and is where the majority of coalmining took place.

BOSTON SPA.   32000

Visitors to the town seem to have been made up from two groups: travellers using the Great North Road who stopped over just long enough to sample the waters in the Pump Room before clattering off to more interesting places; and the citizens of Leeds who made the place popular enough for a daily stagecoach service to operate.

QUEENS STREET, MORLEY, c.1965.
As part of the Heavy Woollen District of Dewsbury and the Spen Valley, Morley suffered during the slump of the 1930s. Between 1924 and 1930 over 46,000 jobs were lost in the woollen textile industry, most of them in Yorkshire.

M149014

QUEENS STREET, MORLEY, *c.*1965. M149009

After the 1930s the next blow to the Woollen District came in the 1960s with the import of cheap Italian heavy-woollen skirtings and coatings. Even after taking transportation costs into account, cheap labour enabled the Italians to undersell heavy-woollen products even in Yorkshire.

MORLEY GRAMMAR SCHOOL, *c.*1965. M149016

In 1966 proposals were put forward to reorganise the education system within 15 years, so that all children aged 11 to 18 years would attend comprehensive schools. In the meantime an interim system was adopted: comprehensives split between those taking 11 to 13 year olds, and those taking 13 to 18 year olds.

Pictorial Memories Collection

A great new range of publications featuring the work of innovative Victorian photographer Francis Frith.

❧ 1998 Titles ❧

County Series		£9.99
1-84125-045-7	Berkshire	
053-8	Buckinghamshire	
024-4	Derbyshire	
077-5	Greater London	
028-7	Kent	
029-5	Lake District	
051-1	Lancashire	
031-7	Leicestershire	
026-0	London	
027-9	Norfolk	
030-9	Sussex	
063-5	West Yorkshire	
025-2	Yorkshire	

Town & City Series		£9.99
010-4	Brighton & Hove	
015-5	Canterbury	
079-1	Edinburgh	
012-0	Glasgow & Clydeside	
081-3	Norwich	
040-6	York	

Country Series		£9.99
1-84125-075-9	Ireland	
071-6	North Wales	
073-2	Scotland	
069-4	South Wales	

Poster Books		£4.99
000-7	Canals and Waterways	
032-5	Derbyshire	
001-5	High Days and Holidays	
036-8	Kent	
037-6	Lake District	
034-1	London	
005-8	Railways	

		£5.99
023-6	Canterbury	
043-0	Derby	

❧ Titles from January to July 1999 ❧

County Series		£9.99	
1-84125-049-x	Warwickshire	March	
047-3	Staffordshire		
057-0	Devon		
067-8	Cheshire		
065-1	Nottinghamshire		
059-7	Cornwall		

1-84125-101-1	Surrey		
095-3	Hampshire		
128-3	Highlands	April	
149-6	Hertfordshire		
130-5	North Yorkshire	May	
150-x	Wiltshire		

Town & City Series		£7.99	
089-9	Maidstone	March	
087-2	Bradford		
083-x	Colchester		
093-7	Dublin		
091-0	Leeds		
105-4	Buxton		
111-9	Bristol		
113-5	Nottingham		
011-2	Manchester		
107-0	Matlock		
009-0	Macclesfield	April	
132-1	St Ives		
008-2	Derby		
133-x	Sevenoaks		
014-7	Newbury		
134-8	Bognor Regis		
144-5	Leicester		
145-3	East Grinstead		
146-1	Newark		

137-2	Sheffield	May	
138-0	Cambridge		
139-9	Penzance		
140-2	Eastbourne		
147-x	Llandudno		
142-9	Torquay		
148-8	Whitby		
159-3	Scarborough	June	
160-7	Faversham to Herne Bay		
164-x	Scilly Isles		
162-3	Dorset Coast		
168-2	Falmouth		
165-8	Newquay		
154-2	Bakewell	July	
163-1	Lincoln		
167-4	Barnstaple		
174-7	Great Yarmouth		
141-0	Blackpool		
207-7	Dartmoor		

WATERTON PRESS, WATERTON ESTATE, BRIDGEND, GLAMORGAN, CF31 3XP.
TEL: 01656 668836   FAX: 01656 668710

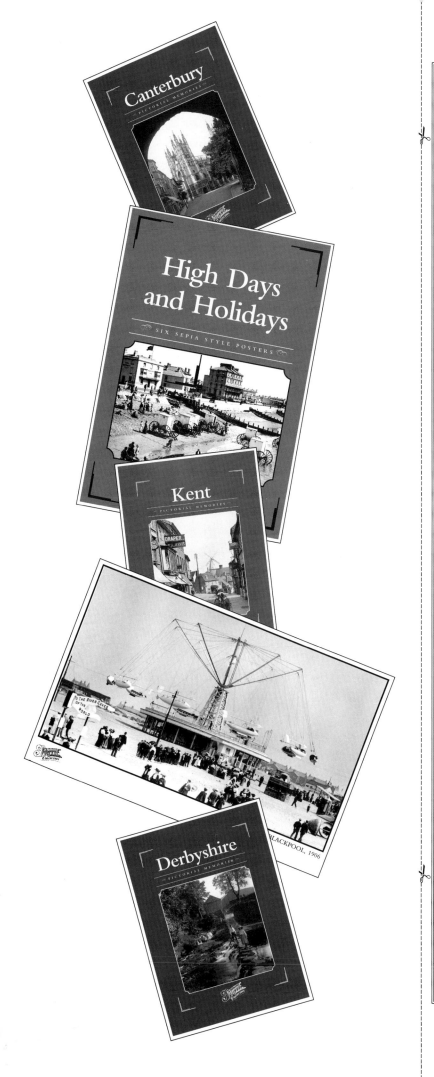